HATS AND CIGARS
Flairing and Pairing

MICHAEL BROWN
The Hat Ambassador

Hats and Cigars
Flairing and Pairing
Copyright © 2021 Michael Brown
All rights reserved.
No portion of this publication may be reproduced, stored in any electronic system, or transmitted in any form or by any means without the written permission from the author. Brief quotations may be used in literary reviews.

DISCLAIMER: **All photographs in this publication were taken by the author.**

ISBN-13: 978-1-7360431-7-2
Library of Congress Control Number: 2021907635

Denola M. Burton
DenolaBurton@EnhancedDNA1.com
www.EnhancedDNAPublishing.com

GREGORY,

Dedication

This book is dedicated to the hat culture and cigar culture.

THANKS SO MUCH FOR THE SUPPORT.
I APPRECIATE IT. ENJOY!

THE HAT AMBASSADOR

10/21/22

Michael Brown

Introduction

There are some things in life that are just supposed to go together. No matter who you are or where you're from, some things are just meant to be. Historically, throughout time, and in every one of our lives, we all know what these things are. Now, it might not be off the top of our heads or even at the tip of our tongues, but when you hear it, you'll know exactly what I'm talking about.

For example, salt and pepper, hot and cold, bacon and eggs, black and white, and even peanut butter and jelly just to name a few. I'll even bet that after reading those, you probably came up with a few of your own, right?

These are just some of the things that we think of as a perfect pair. Two things that perfectly go together, that you can't have one without the other. And for me, if I can add just one more to the list, the absolute most perfect pairing in my book, (pun intended) is without a doubt, hats and cigars! So much so that I incorporated it into my lifestyle. It's even the name of my brand. And so, I felt it was only right to title my first book after my favorite pairing.

So how about we take a look into the world of hats and cigars and really dig deep into this iconic pairing from my perspective.

Michael Brown

Table of Contents

Dedication iii

Introduction v

Chapter 1: Coffee and Trilbies 1

Chapter 2: Boaters and Belvederes 17

Chapter 3: Cognac and Cigars 31

Chapter 4: 3-Pieces and 8-Panels 45

Chapter 5: Fedoras and Flair 57

Chapter 6: Ports and Panamas 77

Chapter 7: Derby's and Dalmore 95

Chapter 8: Top Hats and Two-fingers 107

Chapter 9: Hats and Cigars 121

Chapter 10: Lifestyle and Legacy 125

About The Author 129

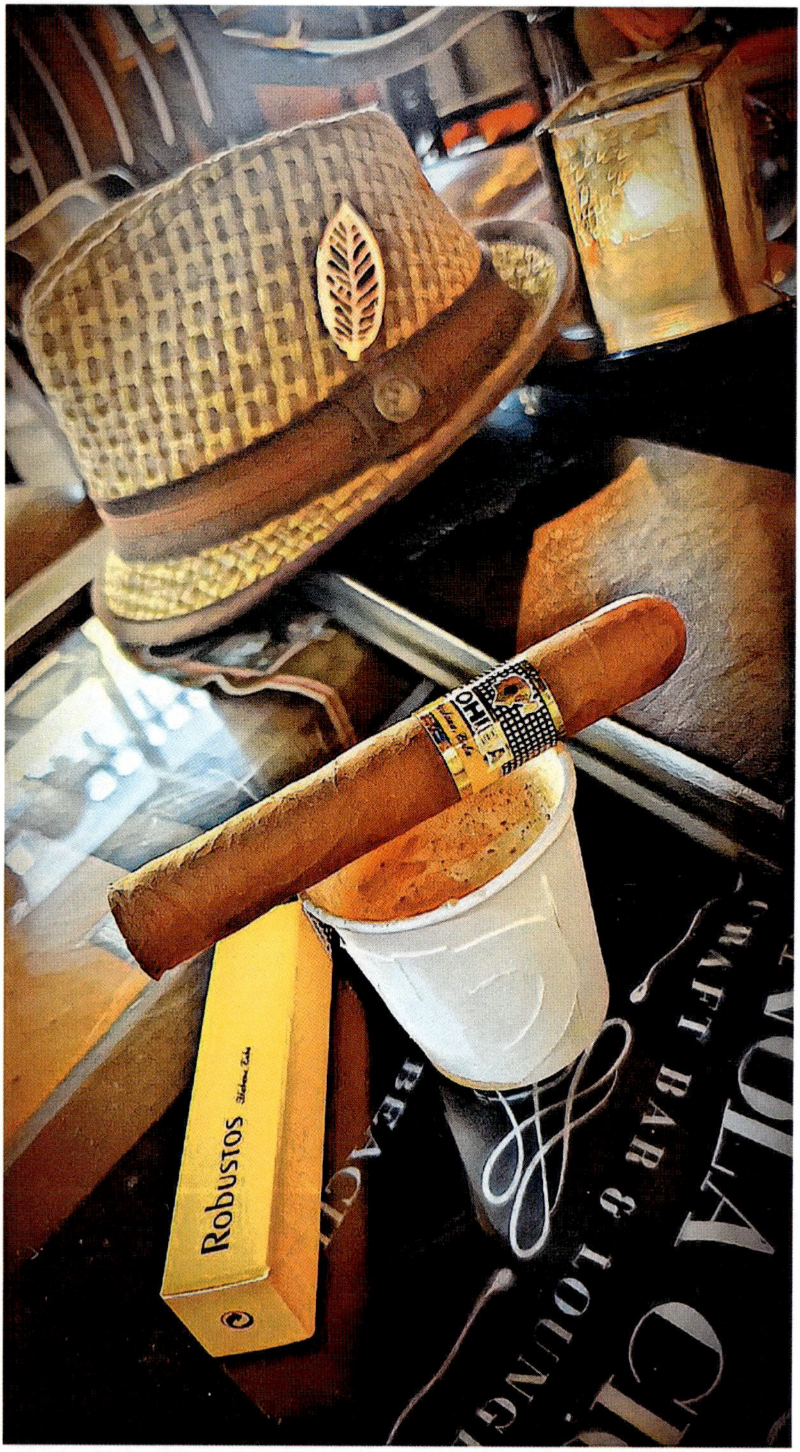
Robustos

Chapter 1: Coffee and Trilbies

"How a hat makes you feel is what a hat is all about"

– Philip Treacy

Every day that I'm blessed to wake up, at some point, I put on a hat. It's my daily routine. It's the life of a hatter and I'd like to believe that I live it like a true hatter should. Of course, we're talking about someone who has over 80 hats and counting. So, it's not an easy task to choose what hat I'll wear on any given day. So, to help make that choice a little easier, it really just comes down to simply how I feel that determines what hat I'm going to wear. I mean…when you put on that hat and take a look in the mirror, you're feeling yourself, that hat just puts a smile on your face, that's what I'm talking about. When a person buys a hat and walks out of the shop proudly wearing it with a smile on their face, that's what I'm talking about. That feeling right there, is what will take you from being a casual hat wearer to a full-fledged hatter.

Now I wouldn't say, by any stretch, that fashion is my thing, but I do feel like I have somewhat of a fashion sense. At least when it comes to my personal fashion. I mean…I've made conscious efforts to come up with my own style. Not that it's anything major. Nothing crazy or too flashy. Actually, quite simple and laid back when you think about it. Just some grown man swag. You know…blazers, V-neck tees, and jeans. I can always dress it up if needed but I do try to look good in anything I wear. Especially when it comes to my hats. Nothing in my wardrobe is complete without a hat to wear with it. You know what they say, when you look good you feel good, and to me, that's what it's all about.

In the back of my mind, I've always felt like, I just decided one day in my forties, that I'm gonna start wearing hats and that was gonna be my thing. Like…it just hit me all of a sudden and I said to myself…man you should start rocking hats. But in all reality, the concept of wearing hats had been ingrained in me at a young age. The funny thing is, it never occurred to me until just a few years ago when I realized that it all made sense to me why I became a hatter.

The majority of people you talk to who wear hats will have their story of what got them into wearing hats. Usually, it was passed down to them or they were influenced by their grandfather or father who wore hats. This is the most common reason I hear of why people wear hats today.

When I think back to my childhood, I remember our living room closet and on the top shelf of the closet, my dad kept his fedoras. Short brim wool fedoras. For him, it was more for function rather than fashion. I remember playing with them as a kid. You know…dress up, trying to look grown. See, my "Pops" always dressed nice. He wasn't into fashion whatsoever, but he was always clean. His job called for it. He was always in 3-piece suits, an overcoat, and a fedora. That's what I remember.

You know, as a kid, you never think of it as something that's cool though. For the most part, most of us probably look at it like…only grown folks wear hats or that's just something "old people" wear. I mean…that's how it was for me. I never really remembered my dad wearing hats having an influence on me when I was coming up, especially since it wasn't until after he passed away that I even started rocking hats. I remember going through his things after he passed and coming across a box full of his old fedoras. Beat up and run down over time but looking at them, seeing them again brought back those memories and I did pause to consider keeping them but at the time, I didn't see a need to do it. Looking back, of course now, I wish I would've kept them, even if only for the sentimental value.

But maybe…everything happens for a reason, right? Because, one day, out of the blue, I finally realized that "Pops" was indeed my inspiration for wearing hats. I mean…maybe this was something that I needed in that moment. Because the timing of it was, it was like, a moment of clarity. As I was walking past one of the wall length mirrors in the shop, I glanced at myself in the mirror and paused. Then I stopped and just took a long look at myself. I mean, literally, self-reflection was happening at that very moment. I had to admire how well I was wearing that fedora. And then, I realized that this wasn't some genius idea that I came up with, but more so the manifestation of something instilled in me many years ago. Maybe it was tucked away in my subconscious somewhere and I just needed this moment to give me the clarity that I needed. So, when I think about it, I guess it all worked out how it was supposed to. If it hadn't of happen this way, I probably wouldn't have the same respect that I do for hats.
Now, it wasn't until I moved to Miami that I got hip to fedoras. And more specifically, trilbies. In Miami they call a trilby the "Cuban" style hat. It was the first hat I bought

in Miami. These hats are prominent up and down Calle Ocho in Little Havana, along with a rich culture, delicious food, and salsa dancing at Ball and Chain. And of course, you can't forget about the dominos, café Cubano (Cuban coffee), and cigars too. It's just part of the whole vibe. So, what is it about the trilby?

The trilby is a hat with a short narrow brim that is turned down in the front and turned up in the back and usually has a shorter crown than a standard fedora. The trilby was at its height in popularity during the 1960's and was one of the signature styles of Frank Sinatra. Typically, trilbies are made from tweed, straw, cotton and wool. It's a great style for someone just getting into hats. People tend to like the style of the trilby and pork pie to start their hat journey due to the smaller brim and shorter crown.

When it comes to styling someone in a trilby there are certain things you want to consider, as with all hats. Head size, first and foremost, face shape, and how someone is built. Meaning, do they have narrow or broad shoulders? Are they short or tall? These are just some of the most common things to consider when choosing a style of hat. Once you've chosen the hat, the only thing left to do is put some flair on it. Don't worry, we'll talk about this in more detail as we get further along.

For me, when I think of a trilby, I think of this hat as a great summer style. That's probably why it's a common style to see in Miami. So, when I think about the Cuban style, I instantly think, a straw trilby worn with a guayabera shirt, linen pants, and loafers. To me, the trilby is just a great all-around casual style that you can wear with a lot of casual looks. And if you're going for that Cuban style, that Miami vibe, it's just not complete without a Cafecito and cigar.

If you ask me, I don't think you can have a much better segue than that, to take us right into our first cigar pairing. I just felt like it was only appropriate to have the first pairing of the book centered around coffee. I mean…since we're talking about Little Havana, trilbies, and café Cubano, why not? Coffee is how millions of people around the world start their day and, if you're inclined to indulge, is great when paired with a cigar.

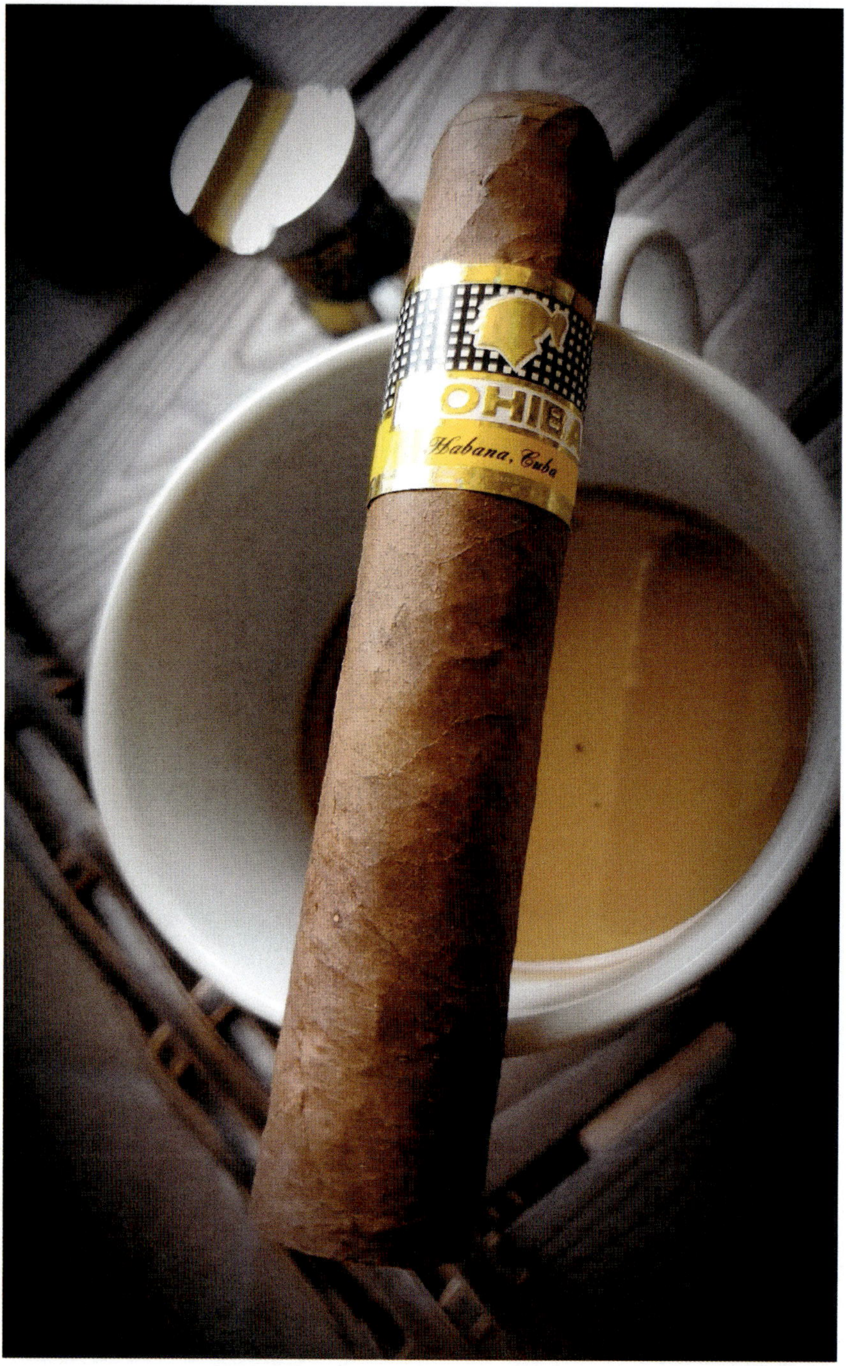
COHIBA
Habana, Cuba

Let's start off first by talking about why this pairing works so well. I feel like the main key element here is that both coffee and tobacco are grown in some of the same regions and countries. Similar soil, similar terroirs, and similar processes which bring out similar flavors. When it comes to complement or contrast, regarding pairing, coffee and cigars complement each other. The goal is to find that perfect balance between the elements that you're pairing. In this case, it's best to pair a mild cigar with a light roast coffee and the same goes for a dark roast coffee and a full-bodied cigar.

For this pairing, we're going to be enjoying some café Cubano and smoking a Cohiba Robustos. Yes! We're smoking a Cuban Cohiba for our first pairing. I mean, it only makes sense, right? The Cohiba Robustos is a perfect cigar to pair with a Cafecito for a couple of reasons. One, being that it's a 5 x 50 ring gauge, smoke time on this cigar is around 45 minutes. So, it's perfect for that first smoke of the day. And two is because, café Cubano comes in small single-serve sized cups which is great when smoking a relatively short stick.

The strength of the Cuban coffee is balanced out by the sweet and smooth flavor of the cigar. To me, the robustos comes off as a medium to full flavored cigar with the fullness coming in more into the last third of the cigar as it seems to get more complex towards the end. Overall, a great and consistent smoke throughout and even better when paired with a café Cubano.

Michael Brown

Hats and Cigars: Flairing and Pairing

as good as memories that you have when you smoked it."

-Raul Julia

Memories. That gets me thinking back to my childhood again. I can't help but to think about someone else who had an influence on me at a young age. Only because he was the first person I had ever seen with a cigar. Mr. Jack Brown (no relation). Mr. Jack was an honest hard-working mechanic who lived in Hannibal, Missouri. Hannibal is where my mom's side of the family is from and is also where my dad was the pastor of a church. One of the deacons at the church and a good friend of my "Pops" was Mr. Jack. Now the reason that he stood out to me is because anytime I ever saw Mr. Jack, he always had the nub of a cigar in the right corner of his mouth. I never remember it ever being lit, but it was always in his mouth. To me, at the time, I just thought he was the coolest cat. He would carry on a conversation and would never adjust or lose that cigar. He just chewed on it I think. But for me, this was my first experience with anyone who smoked cigars and it was one that stayed with me all of these years. You know, even when I look back now and think about it, I realize, that he was just a simple man who loved a good cigar.

Really…that's what it's all about when it comes to cigars for me too. That pure unconditional pleasure that a cigar can give you. Now, it took me many years of smoking to understand this. But I think, that to really accept and appreciate this, it, in fact, takes years to develop. Once I realized this, I felt that I had an obligation to myself to learn as much as I could to better appreciate the experience of smoking a cigar.

I remember the conversation with my boss when she told me that I could take home one cigar from every box in the store and try them. She said I want you to be in charge of the cigars from now on. See…back in the early 2000's, around 2004 maybe, I don't know, I was working at a tobacco shop in Indianapolis. This is where it all started for me and cigars. I quickly took an interest but back then I was just a beginner. I didn't know much but I was eager to learn. This wasn't that long after a new cigar brand had been hitting retailers called Acid. Since I was already smoking Djarum clove cigarettes at that time, an infused cigar was perfect for me. I was drawn to the brand too. I mean, Drew Estate was different. They were cutting edge and trend setters with the infusions and I was all about that vibe. Since then, I've smoked and supported Acid and Drew Estate cigars. They brought me into cigars. It's how I started in the game. But there's always a point in your cigar journey when you want to expand your palate.

When I first heard the term, cigar sommelier, I was instantly intrigued. I mean...I knew what a wine sommelier was, but I never had heard the term, cigar sommelier. I had to know more. What it was all about? What could I do to even become one? But I knew before I could even do anything like that, I would have to change my palate. If I could even, in my own mind, call myself a sommelier, I would have to develop a better understanding and appreciation for the nuances of traditional tobacco. I re-trained my palate, did my research, took the course, and received my certification from IACS (International Association of Cigar Sommeliers). I also knew that this wouldn't, by any means, make me an expert in cigars, but I wanted to at least take advantage of the opportunity to further my education. The more you learn, the more you know and this for me was just part of the journey.

Training as a cigar sommelier focuses on the pairing of cigars and spirits, and more specifically, gourmet pairings. Gourmet pairings are an elevated experience and different than your standard pairing. For the purposes of this book, I'll only focus on standard pairings and we'll dig deeper and explore gourmet pairings further in my follow up book.

I consider a standard pairing as a pairing of two parts, or a 2-part pairing. The cigar is one part, and the spirit is the second part. For the pairings in this book, I've chosen them based on my particular preference and palate. My favorite spirit is cognac. My favorite brand is Hennessy. And so, a lot of my pairings are with different blends of Hennessy. But not just because I like cognac but also because it's a great spirit to pair with cigars. I also have pairings with coffee, scotch, and a port wine as well. See, the key to coming up with great pairings is to have two elements that complement each other in a way that creates a perfect harmony between them. I've considered the aspects and notes of both the cigars and spirits in coming up with what I believe are some great pairings that can be enjoyed by a wide range of aficionados and connoisseurs.

Pairings are not the only aspect of training for a sommelier however it is one of the key principles of being a sommelier and what a sommelier does. Service is the main aspect of a sommelier. Providing an unparalleled experience through service and presentation of a pairing or tasting. It's not just about smoking a cigar and having a drink. It's more to it than that. There is a beauty and elegance to properly preparing and presenting a cigar and spirit for pairing.

I look at this book as a way for me to use my knowledge as a sommelier and share with you some of my favorite pairings. It's like, the best way for me to be able to take what I've learned and present it in the best way possible other than an actual live presentation. And so, for me, and I hope all of you, this book is the next best thing.

Hats and Cigars: Flairing and Pairing

Michael Brown

Chapter 2: **Boaters and Belvederes**

"Cock your hat…angles are attitudes."

– Frank Sinatra

I never knew this was a quote from Frank Sinatra. But when I think about it, it does make sense. This is the kind of advice I would expect to get in his era. I mean…cool is cool, right? And Frank was cool. He was debonair. The way he wore his hats reflected his lifestyle. He had style and attitude. Not to mention, his class and character was appealing to both men and women.

So, it doesn't surprise me that I've heard this quote many times while working at the hat shop. I mean…if Izzy was styling you, you probably heard this advice too. More than likely, he would just cock it for you so you could see the potential in how to wear the hat. And then once you realize that potential, when you can actually see it, the rest will fall into place and come naturally. It's like…every time he says it, I'm thinking…man, that's just the perfect saying. And it's true too! I mean…it just gives you a whole different kind of swag when you put a tilt on it and cock it to the side.

Depending on who you are, the potential of what a hat can look like or how you can wear a hat comes down to, a lot of the time, your confidence. Confidence is key! If you're confident in wearing the hat, it will show. Trust me. A slight tilt of the hat or snap down of the brim can show everyone just how much you own your look. And that's what it's about. Owning it! Remember to always wear the hat, and don't let the hat wear you!

Since I started my hat journey, my hat collection has grown right along with the different styles of hats that I wear. And, as with many people, I too have grown as my journey with hats has grown. Kind of in the same way my palate has grown with cigars. I'm more comfortable now wearing some different styles of hats that I never would've worn before. And it comes with it. It's just all a part of the process and the journey. It's an evolution to this hat game.

One of the best parts of hatting is that there are so many different styles of hats you can wear. There's always gonna be a way to express yourself through a hat. This never-ending relationship we have with hats is a passion that continues to grow with us, especially the more we indulge ourselves. And we just have to, right? There's no reason for it but we still do it. Ironically, it's kind of the same way with cigars and that's why, to me, pairing hats and cigars is undeniable.

I knew that I was becoming a full-fledged hatter when I could finally start wearing a boater. For me, this wasn't an easy task. The boater just wasn't a style of hat that I had liked. Any time that I had tried one on, I just didn't think I wore them well. I wasn't confident enough to pull it off. And remember, I mentioned how confidence is a big part of wearing hats. I've seen plenty of people rock boaters and look good wearing them and I've also sold boaters to a lot of customers, but for me, it took me a year or two before I could really wear this style.

Now…before I get ahead of myself, let's stop and take a closer look at the boater and why now, it's a style that I've added to my repertoire.

Boaters are a straw hat that's considered a semi-formal summer style hat. They were at their height of popularity in late 19th century and early 20th century. The hat is made of a stiffened straw with a stiff flat crown and brim as well. The style of the hat comes from the canotier hats that were worn by gondoliers in Venice, hence the name, boater. And you may also remember them or associate them with barbershop quartets as this was the style of hat worn during that era.

Since the boater is considered a semi-formal hat, similar to that of a Homburg or bowler, it's best to style this hat with a blazer or even a suit and tie. Also, since it is more of a vintage styled hat, vintage looks will always go well with a boater. If you by chance go to any roaring 20's or Gatsby themed parties, think of, women wearing flapper dresses and cloche hats, dancing the Charleston, and the men wearing vintage styled suits and boater hats, smoking a Belvedere.

Hats and Cigars: Flairing and Pairing

Michael Brown

"The best cigar in the world is the one you prefer to smoke on special occasions, enabling you to relax and enjoy that which gives you maximum pleasure."

-Zino Davidoff

I can't think of a single occasion that I couldn't or any occasion that I wouldn't celebrate with a good cigar. See, to me, everyday life is reason enough to celebrate with a smoke.

That's why my daily routine usually consists of getting home from a long day at the shop, pouring a drink, and then lighting up a cigar. This is my favorite way to unwind. It's like, all of the days stresses just escape your body. It gives the mind the peace it needs to recharge. It gives me the chance to reflect on things I did that day and ways I can better myself for the next day. A lot of great ideas spawn from enjoying a good cigar and allowing the mind to take a break from the days' stresses. Kind of like that line from the hip-hop classic, "You Gots To Chill" by EPMD, you know, "relax your mind and let your conscience be free…". Well, to me, I feel like smoking a cigar is a perfect way to relax and indulge yourself. I guess you could call it, smoke therapy. No occasion needed. Maximum pleasure is the desired effect and how you get it is up to you.

Looking out…off the balcony…at times it can be calm and serene and at others it's busy and…well…normal. Either way, it's my spot. Most of the time that I spend enjoying cigars is done, sitting in my chair, on my balcony. It's easy to get lost in the smoke when you have such a beautiful view to get lost in.

During the day the sun shimmers off the water and at night the moon and city lights reflect off of it. Yachts casually pass back and forth on the Intercoastal. Sometimes it's a party going by and sometimes they just anchor to take in a beautiful sunset. Kayaks, paddle boards, and jet skis are common to see. Even the Crew teams get it in too. Every now and then you might see some dolphins playing or a manatee slowly swimming. Sharks are rare…but I have seen one. Then look out to the Atlantic and see the colorful kites of the kite surfers in the ocean. Cruise ships off in the distance. The clouds hug the horizon. Beautiful rainbows appear after afternoon showers. Sunsets reflect off city buildings. Swimmers doing laps in the Olympic pool, sunbathers relaxing, and kids playing. Sirens blare from the firehouse across the water. Most of the time it's beautiful…but sometimes it can be ugly. Pretty much, there's always something happening if you live in Miami Beach!

Sometimes…it's always like this. And sometimes…it's not. But it's my favorite place to hang out at.

"Off the balcony I'm 'bout to be all in the mix…"

I would be remiss if I didn't speak about this right here!

Belvedere. That just sounds like something I'd be into. It fits my vibe you know what I'm saying. It just sounds bougie. But that's why I'm feeling it though. And it wasn't until recently that I first heard the term. I was curious enough that I had to look it up. Do some research. Come to find out, Belvedere is a, not-so common, slang term for a cigar. Not only that, but a Belvedere is also a cigar shape, or "vitola". Meaning, its size is slightly shorter than a Corona which is like a 5 ½ inch long cigar and its ends are thinner than a Corona too which usually has a ring gauge of 42. For example, H. Upmann in Cuba used to make a Belvedere, kind of shaped like a Perfecto, that was machine-made and had a 5 x 39 size to it. I had no idea. But if you ask me, I say we should bring this back into the lexicon of terms for how we refer to cigars. Belvedere. I mean…it just has a classy kind of feel to it to me. And we can never have too much class and sophistication when it comes to the culture.

"I mean…come on now…you already know. We smoke Belvederes over here!"

Most of the time that I spend coming up with a pairing is trying to find the elements that work best together. The ones that give you the best experience throughout the entire pairing. This, by no means, is an easy task. Sometimes, however, a pairing just works. From the first time you try it you know. The cigar. The spirit. They both come together beautifully. The first time that I had our next pairing, it was the same way for me. A perfect pairing in my opinion. So, I definitely wanted to share it with you.

I was on a weekender, going over to the gulf coast of Florida and decided to stop in Naples to have a smoke at Burn by Rocky Patel. It was my first time going to this lounge and I couldn't wait to check it out. Browsing in the humidor, I happened to come across a cigar I hadn't seen before. I had to get it. I mean…I had heard about it, but this would be my first time ever smoking it.

Already being a fan of Drew Estate, I was excited to finally get to smoke a Pappy Van Winkle Family Reserve. First off, the Pappy Van Winkle is amazing right from the moment you hold it to your nose. I was always curious about Drew Estate's fire cured tobacco. The aroma is intoxicating. I feel like the fire cured and barrel fermented tobacco is what does it for me with this cigar. Especially, with it being wrapped in a combination of Mexican San Andres and Kentucky Tapa Negra leaves. Such a beautiful and unique combination that creates a bold flavor profile. I love it! I can easily say that it's my favorite cigar.

I just so happen to order a Hennessy V.S.O.P. to sip on while I enjoyed my cigar. I wasn't even thinking about really pairing them at the time but, to my surprise, they ended up pairing great together.
Now, if you think about it…I wouldn't think that a cigar with tobacco that was fermented and cured in bourbon barrels would pair well with a cognac. I would think that they would contrast each other too much. However, the notes from the bourbon barrels are ever so elegantly subtle that they only come through as a hint of sweetness on the palate. This allows the cigar to marry up beautifully with the sweeter notes of the V.S.O.P. like, in this case, the vanilla and clove that you get on the front of your palate and the caramel notes on the finish. There's also some spice or "bite" that comes in at the end of the Hennessy that finishes off the charred campfire like notes you get when smoking the Pappy Van Winkle.

An undeniable match made in heaven is a perfect way to describe this harmonious pairing. From the first time that I had it, to every other time since then, it's always delivered as an exceptional and satisfying pairing that gives your palate a complex yet equally enjoyable tasting experience. Something I like to call "sophisticated relaxation."

Hats and Cigars: Flairing and Pairing

Michael Brown

Chapter 3: **Cognac and Cigars**

"Cognac and cigars... it's like finding the perfect woman. When you've got her, why go chasing after another?"

-Michael Nouri

My sentiment exactly! I couldn't have said it any better myself. In fact, in my opinion, I'd say the same goes for hats and cigars but since we're talking cognac, let me take this opportunity to share with you my connection with Hennessy and why it's my favorite spirit to pair with cigars.

December 14, 2019, I boarded a plane not knowing what to expect when I landed. I mean, I had a destination, but I wasn't sure of what to do once I got there. I was nervous, anxious, and excited. Little did I know that I was embarking on what would prove to be the trip of a lifetime.

Cognac has been my spirit of choice for years and specifically Hennessy has always been my go-to. The U.S. is currently the #1 market of Hennessy in the world and is primarily due to the hip-hop culture. That's where my love for Hennessy started. Back in the day, in the 90's, as an up-and-coming rapper in the Midwest. Now 25 or so years later, it's still my spirit of choice and it all came together for me in one of the most amazing experiences of my life.

I mean…the opportunity itself was enough to put this experience on an epic level. But more importantly, I was able to meet some incredible people in the process. People that I will refer to as friends for life because we were able to share in something special together. So, needless to say, big shout out to the Brothers of Bagnolet. Much love and much respect bruvs!

This trip for me was a lot of firsts. I don't even know where to start. Let's see…what major bucket list boxes did I check? First time on a flight for 9 hours. First time in Europe. In Paris, France. Seeing the Eiffel Tower. Going to Cognac, France, and getting to tour Hennessy. A definite first and for sure the highlight of the entire experience.

I had the pleasure of enjoying my first cigar of the trip once we arrived in Cognac, France. We had some downtime before dinner, so I felt like it was the best time to have a cigar. I stopped in the hotel bar and got a glass of Hennessy V.S.O.P. then went and sat down in front of the hotel to enjoy the moment and just take it all in. It was the perfect time to sit back, enjoy a good smoke, and just appreciate how blessed of an opportunity it was to be there.

This also happened to be the first chance I had to use some of my cigar sommelier knowledge. It was just a month prior that I took the course, so I was excited to use some of what I had learned. A few gentlemen were outside of the hotel smoking cigarettes and seemed to be intrigued by me and the cigar I was smoking. One of them walked over and chatted me up. It just so happens that cigarette smoking seems to be more common in France which I didn't know. Anyway, I thought it was cool that they were interested, and I was more than willing to share. I explained to them how excited I was to smoke a cigar in France. That due to the unique organic properties of cigars, the taste of it can change depending on where you smoke it. For example, changes in temperature, humidity, time of day, region, or country can all affect how the cigar tastes. So, if you want to have the ultimate experience smoking a cigar, it's best if smoked where the tobacco originated from. This is due to the terroir of the region which brings out the absolute best properties of the tobacco. This is similar in the same way that the grapes to make cognac can only come from the Cognac region in France. The grapes in the region have specific qualities due to the terroir of the region that makes them perfect for making cognac. And let me just say, I was blown away to learn that cognac was made from grapes. I absolutely had no idea. And that's just one of the reasons this trip was so great because I was able to learn so much that I didn't know and gain a greater appreciation for a lot of things that I did know.

I guess now I can finally say that I'm international. Literally! It just so happens I was able to take my brand global, without even really trying to, but it happened. This was the opportunity that gave me a chance to showcase my brand on a whole new level. I could share my story with people I never thought of reaching before and they could experience what Hats and Cigars is all about. This was the chance to introduce The Hat Ambassador to an international market and for that, I'm forever grateful to everyone who made it possible.

So, just to set the scene for you…on a table in the courtyard, a box of Hennessy matchsticks lay next to an ash tray. I used a couple of the matches to light the cigar and put another matchstick in the band of my hat I was wearing. You already know I had to add some flair to my hat with this Hennessy matchstick. See, it's little souvenirs like this or other small keepsakes or mementos that you can use to elevate your hat game and give special meaning to your favorite hat.

Michael Brown

Now, the last part of our tour, on our last night in Cognac, we were able to have dinner at Le Maison de Bagnolet, which is the Hennessy family mansion. Aside from the obvious on why this was so amazing, one of the best moments for me was capping off the most incredible dinner by having a choice of cigar from the house humidor. Humbled by the gesture, I knew this was a once in a lifetime moment. I happened to choose a Zino Platinum Z Class 550 R to pair with the Hennessy XO that was our after-dinner drink. It was my first time trying this cigar and I was definitely pleased with the choice and how well this pairing was.

Ironically, about a year later, I found another pairing with XO that was comparable to this one and that's what I'll be sharing with you now.

This trip just so happened to be the first time I ever had the pleasure of having Hennessy XO. Actually, it was also the first time I had Hennessy Paradis as well. But for this pairing, I'm raising my glass with some XO in it.

XO stands for Extra Old and means that the youngest of the eaux-de-vie used in this blend is at least 10 years old. Eaux-de-vie (*water of life*) is what the wine is called that's used to make cognac. It's a clear colored wine that's distilled twice and then is aged in French oak barrels. This is where the color and the nuances of cognac comes from, the barrels. Once it has been aged in barrels, the eaux-de-vie is then blended to create a particular cognac such as VSOP or XO, for example. The blends used for XO have around 100 different eaux-de-vie that can be anywhere between 10 to 70 years old, making it a deep, rich, and complex expression from Hennessy.

Hats and Cigars: Flairing and Pairing

The true elegance of XO is in the flavors. The subtle and smooth notes of cinnamon, fruit, and vanilla balance out perfectly with the spice and chocolate notes. Such a premium spirit should be enjoyed with an equally premium cigar. And for this pairing I'll be smoking the Zino Platinum Crown Series Limited Edition 2020.

The LE 2020 is a beautiful 5 x 60 Gran Robusto. Nice stick if you like big ring gauges. It's a full-bodied and full-flavored cigar that definitely delivers with rich flavors and an inviting aroma. It's sure to please even the most sophisticated palate. With a smoke time of close to 120 minutes, it gives you plenty of time to explore this complex smoking experience.

From the very beginning of this cigar, you know that you're smoking an excellent representation of what a premium cigar should be. It's just that simple. This one is a winner, hands down. It's packed with flavor and the strength is there, but it's not too strong. The LE 2020 and the XO are perfect when paired together because they're both complex in their own ways. But this works! They both need another partner in the pairing that can handle the other. This way neither of them are overshadowing the other one. They play well together. And that, my friends, makes for an absolute amazing smoking experience that we as smokers can only hope to experience at least once, before it's all said and done.

Hats and Cigars: Flairing and Pairing

"I don't use a hat as a prop. I use it as a part of me."

-Isabella Blow

This right here hits me deep.

"You see...My hat is just as much a part of me as my prescription frames and my hazel eyes behind them. Just as much as my gift of gab and that Indiana twang you hear in my voice. Just as much as my cigar ring. I mean, my hat is just as much a part of me as anything. Just as much as the ink forever on my skin and just as much as the experiences I've been blessed to have in my lifetime. My hat is never a prop! Never that! See…my hat is a part of me like the blood flowing through my veins with that Brown DNA written all over it. Just as much as the ups and downs along the way and just as much as the growth that got me here. My hat is everything! It's just as much a part of me as these words I wrote. Just as much as the dirt under my nails from clawing my way out the streets. My hat is just as much a part of me as my first and my last breath! And I haven't taken my last...yet! That's…how much my hat is a part of me."

I mean...I can't express to you just how much my hat is a part of me but hopefully, in some type of way, you were able to feel me on that!

Hats and Cigars: Flairing and Pairing

Michael Brown

Chapter 4: 3-Pieces and 8-Panels

"People, when they buy a hat, they can't explain why they want to buy it or why they want it, but they do. It's like chocolate."

-Philip Treacy

And who doesn't love chocolate? Pretty much all of us, right? We'll talk about chocolate more in my follow-up title about gourmet pairings. Fortunately, I've been blessed with the opportunity to see this phenomenon first-hand. For the past, almost 4 years now, I've had the pleasure of working for Goorin Bros. hat company at their retail shop in South Beach, Miami, Florida. And before that, I was also a customer at the very same shop. So, I've actually experienced this from both sides. As someone who loves and buys hats, to someone who sells hats and loves to help customers experience that same feeling.

The first time I walked in to a Goorin Bros. shop was my first time ever being in a hat shop. The idea was foreign to me in a way. I had never seen anything like it where I was from. Now, I can expect to find hat shops in bigger cities, larger markets, but for me, this was all new. It was a kid in a candy store type vibe for me. All of the hats that I had up to this point were all bought online. And you know how that is. Sometimes it's hit and miss as far as fit goes and how it looks once you put it on. So, it was actually refreshing to have a shop to go into and try on hats. The most important thing when buying a hat is how it fits. So, when you can try on several styles and get a feel for what fits and what doesn't, both in size and looks, it's crucial. And ultimately, it will probably lead to you buying the hat that fits and looks the best.

I mean...working on Lincoln Road, just the location itself puts you in the heart of South Beach. But also, the vibe, the atmosphere, and the people. The opportunities have been an added bonus that I never imagined would happen. Needless to say, landing in this spot has truly been a blessing to me and I'm grateful to have landed here. I mean...it's been the first place that I've worked that it was encouraged to come to work with your own style. And where you can rock hats every day that accompany and accent that style. This is where my hat game really flourished. I was quickly converted from wearing flat caps to rocking fedoras once I moved to Miami.

Before that, years ago, I made a conscious effort to start wearing flat caps. I knew that I wanted to add hats to my repertoire, and at the time they were a good look for me. I mean, I was rocking duckbill ivy's, Kangols, 1-panel flat caps, and even the Peaky Blinders style before it was poppin'. I even had a flat cap for winter that had the ear flaps and attached to the top of the cap by a button. It's definitely my go-to when it gets cold. I mean...I think I've got about 30 or so flat caps in my entire collection.

Flat caps are also commonly referred to as ivy caps, driver caps, and newsboy caps. They are generally made from wool, cotton, and most commonly, tweed but also come in linen and sometimes straw. One of my favorite flat caps that I use to have was even made from a coffee sack!

The reason for the different names or styles of caps is because of the way they are cut or made. Ivy and driver caps are usually made with one, three, or six panels of fabric that make the hat, with the most common flat cap, typically being a 6-panel ivy. Another popular style of flat cap is the newsboy cap or sometimes referred to as a paper boy or gatsby. This flat cap has 8 panels of fabric which gives it a looser fit so the wearer can style it to one side or the other.

Even more recently, due to the popularity of a certain series, some flat caps are associated with or sometimes referred to as a "Peaky Blinders" cap. The huge success of the show has given flat caps a comeback in the hat game. Before, they were looked at as more of an "old man's" style. Now, flat caps are trending and more people are wearing them. It's not just an "old man's" hat anymore.

You know…it kind of makes sense that I started out wearing flat caps because at the time I was just a casual hat wearer and I feel like, the flat cap is the perfect casual hat. Of course, you can dress it up too, but in its essence, to me, it's one of the most casual styles of hat you can wear.

Look wise, you can easily wear a flat cap with a t-shirt and shorts or maybe like a polo and khakis. I like to think of or associate a flat cap with golf for some reason. To me, it just seems like it works with that type of style and fashion and it feels like they go together. If you remember, Samuel L. Jackson famously wore Kangol golf caps with his signature style of wearing the cap backwards so you could see the brand logo.

If you do dress up a flat cap, I suggest styling it with a suited look or something similar. Vintage looks will always go well with a newsboy cap. Again, think of Peaky Blinders or even The Great Gatsby for those good vintage styles that work with a cap. You know, something like, a 3-piece suit and tie combo. Maybe, even wear just the vest and go with a bowtie for a different look. Or change it up with something like suspenders, an ascot, and wingtips. Then complement that look with a matching 8-panel.

Hats and Cigars: Flairing and Pairing

Michael Brown

"Cigar smoking knows no politics. It's about the pursuit of pleasure, taste, and aroma."

-- Anonymous

The perfect example of this, to me, is any of the many cigar lounges throughout the world. I mean…I love going to lounges. I love traveling and going to different lounges. When I walk into a lounge, the first thing I notice is the beautiful aroma of the tobacco from all the cigars that were smoked there before me. It's a smell that you never forget and one that you always welcome. At least I do.

I'm originally from Indianapolis, Indiana. Born and raised. I lived there for 44 years. Before I moved to Miami in 2015, Indianapolis only had one cigar lounge, Nicky Blaines. Needless to say, there wasn't much of a cigar culture even back then. See…one of the benefits of moving to Miami was going from a city with little to no cigar culture to a city with a robust and thriving cigar culture. Fast forward to now, the culture is growing in Indianapolis and that's evident by the fact that there's now a total of four cigar lounges. Nicky Blaines, as I mentioned, Burn by Rocky Patel, Blend by Davidoff, and Stixx. All great lounges.

The ambiance of a lounge is what does it for me. Maybe you could even say, its character. Different lounges have different character to them. Whether it's just your normal small neighborhood lounge or an elegant upscale spot, each has its own vibe. And I'm fine with both, and everything in between for that matter. I love getting to know what that vibe is. You know what I'm saying? I mean…I like to walk into a lounge and just pause for a minute. You know, peep things out. See how the place is set up. And then make my way to the humidor. I can get lost in a humidor. There's just something about it. The smell of the cedar. The smell of the cigars. I just want to explore the humidor and see what that selection looks like.

The lounge is where you can truly get lost in a ritual that's forever timeless. Whether it's the sounds of soft jazz soothing your ears, or it's just the solace of being in a place where everyone knows your name. It can be the exceptional service, and believe me, service is key. Or maybe it's just the fact that it's a place for you to take a couple of hours and enjoy some peace and tranquility. The lounge is where you can strike up conversations with strangers, where you can meet up with friends, and where you can end up as family. The lounge is where you can fellowship with other people from every walk of life imaginable. All because of the one common thing that we all have between us when we're at the lounge, and that's cigars.

It's amazing to me how cigars can bring people together in the way that they do. What I mean is, and anyone who smokes knows what I'm talking about. But there's like…this unspoken bond that we all have. We already know, there's this one thing that we all have in common. Just starting from that in itself, already breaks down all kinds of walls between whomever you may have the pleasure of smoking with. I mean…without even knowing who you are, if you smoke cigars…you alright with me. But it's just that thing. That thing that we all have between us. That one thing that brings us all together. So really, when it comes down to it, there's no politics when it comes to cigars.

Being in the culture now for several years, I feel like the best thing about cigars is that you're always on a never-ending pursuit for the pleasure in which they bring you. When you find that pleasure, when you hit that sweet spot, you automatically know it. What's so intriguing and fun about this pursuit, is that you'll always find new and exciting ways to please your palate. I say do it! I encourage you to explore and seek out the endless choices available to you. To partake in something which is so carefully crafted and provided for you so that you can indulge and please yourself. Go and expand on what you know and learn as much as possible. Enhance the culture. Enrich the culture. Elevate the culture.

Hats and Cigars: Flairing and Pairing

Michael Brown

Chapter 5: **Fedoras and Flair**

"My aim is to change people's perceptions of what a hat can look like in the 21st century."

– Philip Treacy

This! This right here is one of the reasons that I became The Hat Ambassador. I just had this feeling like, I knew I could bring my own swag and flair to the hat culture and through that, hopefully inspire people to wear and flair their own hats.

What I wanted to do, or hoped to do, is add some value to the hat culture by being an ambassador of hat fashion and style. Hopefully to bring awareness to wearing a hat for more than function, but more importantly, for the fashion of it. Inspire people to look at hats in a different way. Especially, right now with how much of an outlet that social media is, with hat groups and influencers, there's so many people are out here rocking hats and representing the hat culture more than ever. And let me just say, that Miami is a perfect city to live and be able to fashionably wear hats? And there couldn't have been a better opportunity for me to do this than working for a hat company.

See…I interact with people on a regular basis who have their own preconceived perceptions about wearing hats. Now, it's not my job to change their mind, but it does give me an opportunity to use my experience and knowledge to help educate people. And that's what I'm trying to do. As an ambassador. As someone who represents the culture. See, I look at it as my contribution to the culture. Educating those who want to learn more about hatting. And there's a lot that I've learned about hats working for Goorin Bros. And to that point, one of the most important aspects of hatting that I've learned, without a doubt, is flairing your hat. I mean…it's in the title of the book. So…let's just get right into it. Because I know y'all are probably like…

Flairing? WTF is flairing? Well…here's the definition.

Flair
/fler/
noun

2. Stylishness and originality.

"He dressed with flair."

Hats and Cigars: Flairing and Pairing

When I first started working at the shop and was just getting into fedoras, I would always wear my hats "clean" - meaning, just the hat. No feathers. No pins. Nothing. No flair whatsoever. One of my co-workers would always encourage me to add feathers and pins to my hats to incorporate my own personal style to it. And I've got to admit, once I started flairing out my hats, that was it! The word "flair" was officially a part of my vocabulary.

The beautiful thing about flairing your hats is that there are no rules. Because when it comes down to it, all you're doing is adding your own flair to the hat. Your own personality. It's a way to make the hat your own. Meaning, you're adding your own personal flair to it. You can go for a simple clean look or you can go as wild and creative as you want. It's up to you and what type of look or statement you want to make with your hat.

The feather is the most common and traditional type of flair you can add to a hat. They're by far the most versatile piece you can add to give your hat some flair. There are countless options and combinations to choose from when it comes to feathers. They come in a variety of sizes and colors. Whether you add just one or you add several of them, feathers will always add a nice touch to any hat.

The more that hats are accepted as fashion pieces, the more opportunity there is to flair hats so that they stand out. That also means more things that you will see used to flair out a hat. Just some of the things that I can think of that I've seen are, matchsticks, playing cards, buttons, flowers, safety pins, and even porcupine quills to name a few. But pretty much anything you can think of, when it comes down to it, you can probably add it to a hat and flair it out.

Michael Brown

With more and more people now getting into the hat game, you're also seeing a growth in customizing hats. I also look at this as flairing a hat too. Now, I do want to say that customizing a hat is not the same as a custom-made hat. Customizing is done to an already existing hat while a custom-made piece is just that, a custom-made hat created from scratch. With that said, people are now adding elements to hats like paint or adding other textiles like cloth or leather. Changing up the bands. Stitching in designs with threading or even branding or burning a design into a hat. I mean…it's even common now for people to set a hat on fire to get a distressed look to it. All of these things and more are possible if you want to add some flair to your hat.

Hat pins! Now, hat pins are my thing. I feel like, next to feathers, hat pins are another common type of flair you'll see on most hats. Just like feathers, there are a variety of sizes and styles of hat pins. Most hat pins you see will be soft enamel pins. However, there are other styles as well such as hard enamel, 3D dye cast, and full color pins. Another type of hat pin that I'm a big fan of is the vintage hat pin. These pins usually have a long straight pin that has a decorative or ornamental tip.

Inspiration can come in many forms. Funny how that works. See…the seed was planted for me one day at the shop when a gentleman came in looking to get a couple of hats. Sharp brother. Preston, out of Charlotte. We happen to get on the topic of cigars and come to find out, he's the owner of a couple of cigar lounges in Charlotte too. So, I'm working on styling his hat and he asks if we sell any cigar hat pins which I explained that we didn't. After that I really didn't think much of it until I just so happen to run into this BOTL *(Brother Of The Leaf)* again a few months later at the

Miami Mega Herf Cigar Yacht Party. He asked me again about the cigar hat pins and I had to tell him that we didn't carry anything like that at the shop. I followed that up by admitting that I didn't think that there even was a cigar hat pin on the market. This time though…I made the effort and did some research. After the event, I went home, opened the laptop, and started looking for cigar hat pins. I mean…was there even such a thing as a cigar hat pin? Was anybody already making something like this? To my surprise…there wasn't! Nobody was doing it. Right then, I knew, this is what I was gonna do.

Five months later I received my first shipment of hat pins. I couldn't believe it. My vision had materialized into a business and now my brand was finally tangible. This idea of mine had grown into an actual product. It was real. Hats and Cigars was official!

The Hats and Cigars Logo Pin was the first pin of the collection. I wanted to first establish the brand and what the identity would be going forward and then my plan was to continue expanding the collection. Over the course of two years, I'm proud to say, Hats and Cigars has over 12 pins and is always on the never-ending pursuit to add fresh new pins and other products to the collection.

So…why hats and cigars though? You don't sell hats or cigars. Yeah, yeah, I know. The hat pins are for "hats" and these hat pins are all "cigar" related. That's where the name, Hats and Cigars, comes from. Not to mention, these two things are just simply, a perfect pairing. I wanted to build a business that centered around the two cultures.

Hats and Cigars: Flairing and Pairing

The hat culture and the cigar culture. They go together. Perfectly! Cigar-centric hat pins. Hat accessories. Books. Cigar events. Collabs. Cigar and spirit pairings. You name it. All of this and more is what my vision of the Hats and Cigars lifestyle is all about.

One of the main components of this lifestyle is, of course, hats. I mean…it's the first part of the brand name. It's a crucial piece to the whole thing. A lot of my experience is in hats. It's what I do. I'm The Hat Ambassador! So, let's talk about what I would consider the most common and recognizable hat style there is.

As I mentioned earlier, I started wearing fedoras a few years ago. Now…it's by far my favorite style of hat. I'd say fedoras are about 95% of my hat collection. A lot of people don't know that the fedora was named after woman and that women were the first to wear this style of hat back in the late 1800's. It wasn't until years later that men were predominantly the ones wearing fedoras and women started wearing other styles. There's so much history when it comes to fedoras, however I won't bore you with a history lesson. Instead, how about we take a quick look at what makes a fedora a fedora.

The easiest way to define a fedora is, any hat that is indented, or has what's called a "pinch", in the front of it. You know, the creases on the side. So, for example, that's gonna rule out, porkpie's, boaters, bowlers, homburgs, top hats, and any other hats with an "open" crown. This is like the most general way to look at it. To get into even more detail, we can look at some of the other factors that also distinguish a fedora.

There are two other common aspects about fedoras that are used to categorize them, crown shape and brim width. Crown shape is identified by the crease in the top of the hat as well as the height of the crown, which is normally 4.5 inches for fedoras. The most common type of crown shape that you'll see is called a center dent crown. This crease runs lengthwise down the top of the hat. Another common crown shape is called a teardrop crown. It's called this because of the rounded crease which comes to a point. When you look at the top of the crown, it will look like an upside-down teardrop.

Fedoras are made from all types of materials. Wool, being the most common. Sometimes they're even made with animal felts like beaver and rabbit. Straw, which is my favorite, is also common to make fedoras with. But also cotton, hemp, linen, and leather too.

Now…when we start getting into brims and brim width, that's a whole different conversation, but we definitely have to talk about it.

Short, medium, and wide are all different ways to describe the brim of a fedora. A short or "stingy" brim fedora has a brim that's around 1.5 inches wide or less. The brim is usually worn up all the way around the hat, but you can also wear it down in the front which is more like the trilby style. Small sized feathers or hat pins are best when it comes to flairing out a short brim fedora.

A medium brim is the size you will usually see on most fedoras. This classic brim size is generally 2 - 2.5 inches wide. The traditional way of wearing a fedora is with the brim down in front and up in back but a more modern take is with the brim up all the way around. For the most part, medium brim fedoras will have what's called a "snap" brim, which means you can "snap" it down or "snap" it up to suit your preference. With fedoras, you will usually see a more traditional type of flair. A single small or medium sized feather will always give you that classic look. But you can add more feathers or some hat pins to give it as much flair as you want

Now, when you start getting into brims that are 2.75 inches or wider, that's when we start getting into wide brim fedoras. Wide brims are definitely on trend right now. People seem to be more open to trying a wider brim now than they have in the past and it's a welcomed sight in the hat culture. Typically, wider brims are stiffened so that they hold their shape and retain a flatness to them. The look of the brim has a lot to do with how well the hat looks. And when it comes to flairing out a wide brim hat, I always like to say, as the brims get wider the feathers get bigger.

I've got all sizes of brims in my collection, but it wasn't until, I'd say, in the past year or so that I started wearing some wide brim fedoras. It's taken me years to find some wide brim styles that I felt I could pull off. But, like I said, it's all part of the process. Again, confidence is key. You just have to find it. But when you do, you know it. Every time you can push yourself to step outside the box and try something different, something you're not use to, and you find yourself eventually being able to pull it off…that's what I call…elevating your hat game!

"The cigar is a great resource. It is necessary to have traveled for a long time on a ship to understand that at least the cigar affords you the pleasure of smoking. It raises your spirits. Are you troubled by something? The cigar dissolves it. Are you subject to aches and pains (or bad temper)? The cigar will change your disposition. Are you harassed by unpleasant thoughts? Smoking a cigar puts one in a frame of mind to dispense with these. Do you ever feel a little faint from hunger? A cigar satisfies the yearning. If you are obsessed by sad thoughts, a cigar will take your mind off of them. Finally, don't you sometimes have some unpleasant remembrance or consoling thought? A cigar will reinforce this. Sometimes they die out, and happy are those who do not need to relight too quickly. I hardly need to say anything more about the cigar, to which I dedicate this little eulogy for past services rendered."

-- The Duc de la Rochefoucauld-Liancourt

Hats and Cigars: Flairing and Pairing

Beautifully stated. I mean…that pretty much sums it up right there. Like…think about it. Truer words have never been spoken. This, in a nutshell, is everything that a cigar is. It truly encompasses exactly the way I feel about cigars. This beautiful handmade product that we so humbly get to consume and enjoy, is all of these things…and so much more.

You know, it's funny to me how a cigar can be everything…rolled into one single thing. Think about that for a minute.

This one thing…no matter the size, shape, brand, or price…can cheer you up when you're down. This one thing…can brighten your day if you've been having a rough week. See, this one thing…can find you happiness if you're feeling sad. This one thing…has closed some of the biggest deals. See, this one thing…is how I like to relax after a long day at work. This one thing…can put your mind at ease. This one thing…takes time to become itself and therefore you should always take time to enjoy it. This one thing…can have so many different blends that we'll always have new ones to discover. See, this one thing…can cause two strangers to strike up a conversation. This one thing…is what the culture is all about. It's this one thing…that makes us all brothers and sisters of the leaf. And I'll say it again, this one thing…is the one thing that, to me, is absolutely everything!

That's why I like to take my time when smoking a cigar. See…the time taken to sit and enjoy a cigar is some of the best time spent in my opinion. If I light it…I finish it. Simple as that. I've just always been that way. No need to rush. The point is…to enjoy it! To indulge yourself…in a ritual that has been going on since back when Columbus discovered the Tainos in Cuba and was introduced to tobacco. That's why I take my time. Because of every other hand that's touched that cigar through the entire process to get it into my hand…that's why! See, I'm talking about from seed to cigar! And it's normal for anywhere up to 300 hands to have touched that cigar from start to finish. So, I take my time…out of respect for the leaf!

Michael Brown

Hats and Cigars: Flairing and Pairing

Michael Brown

Chapter 6: Ports and Panamas

"Accessories are key - nothing beats a cool Panama hat or statement shades..."

-Poppy Delevingne

One of the perks of living in Miami is that I have the pleasure of being able to wear a panama hat pretty much year-round. I may rock a wool hat a handful of times in the winter but for me, it's mostly panamas. I'd say probably 85% of my hat collection are panamas or other straw hats. The main reason for this is because out of all the Goorin shops, Miami carries the most straw styles. It does make sense though. A hat shop on the beach, the weather, the sun, and there's no better straw hat for sun protection than a panama. They are rated 50+ UPF. So, when it comes to fashion and function, whether you're at the beach or at the pool, you can't go wrong with a panama. Now, before I started working at the shop, I didn't know anything about panamas, but I quickly learned what makes a panama a panama.

Panamas are universally regarded as the finest of straw hats. The legend of the panama hat is naturally associated with an elegant and refined lifestyle. It just possesses a classic and timeless look. The natural tones of the straw with the simple band of black cloth has become a classic symbol of elegance.

So, what is it that makes a hat a Panama? There are two criteria for a hat to be considered a Panama. It must be hand woven in Ecuador and it must be made with toquilla straw. If so, the hat is considered an authentic Panama.

Hats and Cigars: Flairing and Pairing

> The quality of a montecristi is measured by the fineness of its weave and the rows in its crown.

After that, there are several other factors that are taken into consideration to determine the quality of a panama. A panama can vary in quality depending on, the straw chosen, the expertise of the weaver, and the time spent creating it.

There is somewhat of a grading system with panamas that can help with determining the quality, however, there is no standardized grading that all panamas are measured by, so it's pretty much all subjective. Generally speaking, panamas are graded by the number of weaves in the hat as well as the tightness of the weaves. This means that the grades can range anywhere from a grade 5 up to a grade 30, or higher. So basically, the higher the grade the better the quality.

There's also different types of weaves that can be used to make a panama. The two that I know about are called the Cuenca and Brisa weaves. The Cuenca weave looks like a herringbone pattern while the Brisa weave looks like small diamonds or square shapes in the weave. These are the ones that I'm familiar with.

The highest-graded panama that we've had at the shop was a 35 grade. Beautiful piece! The highest-grade that I have in my collection is a 23 grade. It's definitely one of my favorite hats. The finest panama that I personally have. Since it is one of my favorites, I had to make sure that I flaired it out with a Helmer hat feather. Actually, I think it might have been the first Helmer feather that I bought. You know, I do have to say, when I really want to make a statement with a beautiful quality feather in my hat, my go-to is always Helmer hat feathers.

Hats and Cigars: Flairing and Pairing

When it comes to panamas, there's no better quality than the Montecristi panama. Montecristi's are the crown jewel of panamas. They are regarded as such all over the world. Since its first appearance, the Montecristi panama has symbolized elegance. The quality and beauty of the craftsmanship that goes into a Montecristi can make it warrant a price tag well into the thousands and take several months if not years to weave a hat of this caliber. Only a master weaver will have the skillset required to weave a Montecristi.

There are several different ways to wear or style a panama too. Especially since there's a wide variety of hats that fall under this style. Everything from small to wide brims. From casual styles to a more dressed up style. From porkpies to gauchos to gamblers and even vintage style colonial panamas. Different colors, styles, shapes, and quality. Even with all the possible differences between them, one thing still remains the same…it's a panama!

Panamas, however, aren't the only type of straw hats available in the market. Straw hats can be woven from different types of straw or different straw-like materials that come from other plants or synthetic materials. For example, I have a hat in my collection that's made from polypropylene. By using this material, it makes the hat waterproof. It happens to be one of my favorite hats too. There's also paper, palm, and raffia straw too. Shantung straw, wheat straw, and there's also hats being made from hemp. I have some nice hemp pieces in my collection. Several different colors and I like it because it's a very durable material. I know there's a lot of options available when you're talking about straw hats. So, my suggestion is, if you're looking to get a quality spring or summer style, you can never go wrong with an authentic panama as your go-to piece. Panamas are just simply a style that will never go out of fashion.

It makes me think about something that I never really thought about until I was working at the hat shop. And that's…quality. Quality has a way of showing itself through both, hats and cigars. I didn't realize how much quality mattered until working in the hat industry and having a better appreciation of the hand-made aspects of making hats as well as the materials that are used which can make them a higher quality product. I mean…I've studied this enough that now, I can look at a hat and see whether or not the quality is good. Coincidentally, I feel like the same applies to cigars when it comes to quality too as with most things. Quality can be measured in all things that we indulge in. Just the same as it applies with spirits, it applies to wines too. Quality is quality!

Michael Brown

Hats and Cigars: Flairing and Pairing

"A good cigar is like tasting a good wine: you smell it, you taste it, you look at it, you feel it - you can even hear it. It satisfies all the senses."

-- Anonymous

I can totally understand this and how a keen eye can see some of the similarities between cigars and wine even though you don't hear about them much as a pairing. But I do get it, just in the same way that you examine a glass of wine before you drink it, you also examine a cigar before you smoke it. But the similarities just don't stop there. Both the tobacco grown to make cigars and the grapes used to make wine are grown in a similar way. Meaning that to get the best grapes or the best tobacco, you need to have the best terroir. Which is the soil, the climate, the region it's grown in. All of these things play their part in that cigar you're smoking or that wine you're drinking.

I remember everybody getting their individual pics taken. It was a proud moment. Holding our diplomas. Feeling accomplished. A sigh of relief passing over all of us that we had done it. Once that was done then we all took a group picture. Everybody smiling, happy, the vibe was awesome. I mean…we had just completed our cigar sommelier course. It was time to celebrate!

There was a guy that took the course with me. He was a member at the lounge too. So, he goes back to his locker and comes out with a box of Cuban Cohibas and begins passing them out as a celebratory smoke for all of us. The manager of the lounge, he took the course with us too, he goes and gets a bottle of port wine to have with our cigar. I don't remember the brand, but I do remember how well it paired with the cigar. I was pleasantly surprised. It stuck with me. This was my first experience pairing a cigar and wine.

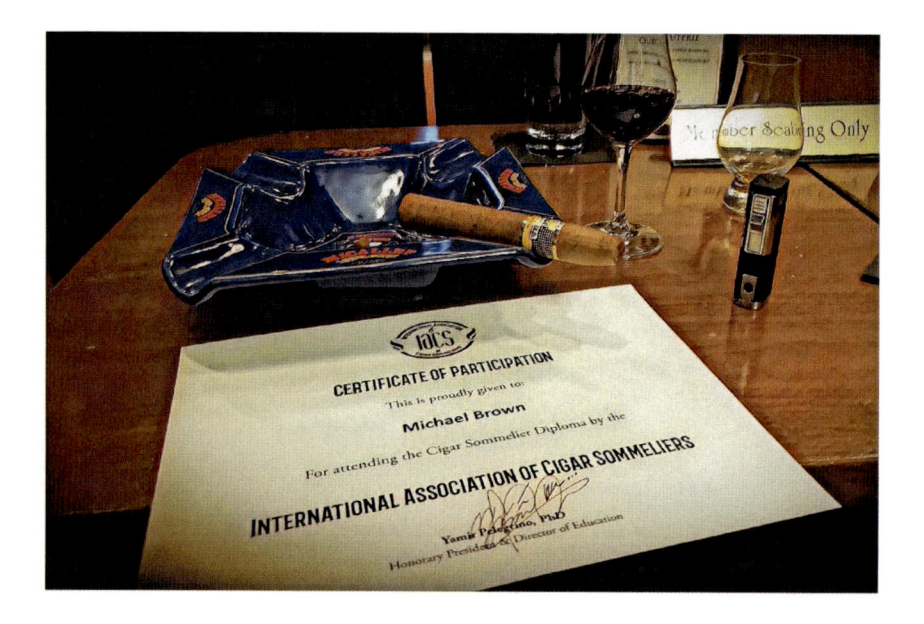

So, I wanted to revisit a cigar and wine pairing for the book. But as far as pairing wine with cigars goes, I'm going to stay with port wines. Especially since that was my first experience with wine and cigars and because, to be honest, I haven't found a better pairing yet for wine and cigars.

The brand of port that currently suits my palate the best is, Quintas das Carvalhas. I like their 10-year tawny port as well as their Late Bottle Vintage 2015. I've acquired the taste and now I'm excited to explore port wines further.

Especially pairing them with cigars. And for this pairing, I'm going with another Cuban.

QUINTA DAS CARVALHAS
THIS IS ONE OF THE OLDEST QUINTAS IN THE DOURO VALLEY, AS WELL AS ONE OF THE BEST LOCATED.
WRITTEN REFERENCES ABOUT QUINTA DAS CARVALHAS DESCRIBING ITS PROMINENT POSITION ON THE LEFT BANK OF THE DOURO RIVER CAN BE TRACED BACK TO 1759
QUINTA DAS CARVALHAS
750ml ℮
10 YEAR OLD TAWNY PORTO
MATURED IN WOOD
PRODUCT OF PORTUGAL

Michael Brown

The best cigar, for me, to pair with the 10 year port is a cigar from a small boutique brand called Dreams of Cuba Cigars. It's the only un-banded cigar I've used for any of the pairings in the book. This cigar is just so good that I had to include in one of my pairings. It's a farm rolled Cuban called the Auntie. This cigar is very limited and only available every so often. It's a 5 x 60 ring gauge and is labeled as a short gordo. It does come in different sizes but this one is my favorite. One of the best Cuban cigars I've ever smoked, in my opinion.

Sidenote…another Dreams of Cuba farm rolled Cuban, the Hector, also pairs amazingly well with the LBV 2015 from Quintas dal Carvalhas.

So…this pairing, for me, is one of the most relaxing. I think the wine element adds a more sophisticated and refined vibe to it.

Michael Brown

Hats and Cigars: Flairing and Pairing

The pace seems to slow down and give you the time to enjoy the notes and nuances between both the cigar and the wine. Wine is complex. It's complex enough to hold its own. It doesn't need a cigar to match its complexity. It pairs best with a cigar that is mild to medium and can balance out the pairing rather than over-power it.

In this case, I found that both the wine and the cigar are medium strength and that's why I feel like they match up beautifully with each other. The first thing that I notice from the cigar is the creaminess of the wrapper. From my experience, this creaminess is a note that you'll commonly get from Cuban cigars with a lighter shade wrapper. I guess it's just in the tobacco. It seems like each region that grows tobacco has characteristics about the tobacco that it's known for. For example, the pepper notes in tobacco from Nicaragua or the strength of the ligero leaves used in the Dominican Republic.

From the first sip of the port wine, it's sweet…but not too sweet. It hits just right on the palate and has a long finish. I could even say that it comes across as full-bodied, to me, for some reason. Maybe due to the robust flavors it has or the complex notes that I get from it. I don't know. The notes are just so perfectly mellow and well balanced but that's why I think it pairs delightfully well with this cigar.

The thing about Cuban cigars for me is that I never really find them to have much complexity to them. Don't get me wrong though, they're great to smoke. To me, I feel like they're consistent when it comes to the flavor profile, but the flavors just don't really change much throughout the smoke. This Cuban Auntie has been consistently good every time that I've smoked it and why it's one of my favorites.

It's smooth all of the way through and that smoothness helps tone down the acidity in the wine. I would describe this pairing as complementary. The cigar and the wine complement each other to the point that the port never overpowers the cigar and the cigars' creamy smoothness keeps the balance between the two like they were made for each other.

Michael Brown

Chapter 7: Derby's and Dalmore

"I can wear a hat or take it off, but either way it's a conversation piece."

-Hedda Hopper

This is so true. And I laugh when I say it because, it's taking on a life of its own. I mean…what I'm saying is, to be The Hat Ambassador, well, part of that attractive character is the hat. It really doesn't work without it. The hat is the key piece. And really the only piece that anyone even cares about. But that's the point. See, that's my whole purpose. To bring an awareness to wearing hats. I mean…I'm trying to bring hatting back! You know, also add in the element of fashion with it and consistently represent that every day. And I feel like because of that commitment to the culture, the expectations are to see me in a hat every time you see me. So…if you just so happen to ever see me without a hat on, then I'd definitely say that is a conversation piece!

Really though, I don't even feel right if I'm not wearing a hat. It's like…you know…you wear a hat so long that you forget you're even wearing it. That's me! Wake up…put a hat on. Go to sleep…take my hat off. Needless to say, only those who are really close to me or in my immediate circle and network have seen me with my hat off. Not like it's a privilege or anything, I'm just saying that it's rare for me to not have on a hat. That's why I love working for a hat company, because I get to wear hats on a daily basis. You'll never see me out in public without a hat on. It's like...you know how on your social media account it says, "Public Figure"? Well...when you're out here day to day representing, when you're out here at the lounges, at the cigar events, and even when you're just representing on social media, because of the amount of access people have to you, you are a public figure. When people see me, they say, *"that's the hat guy"* or it's like, *"that's the guy with the hat pins."* Or *"You know, that's the Hat Ambassador."* Regardless, no matter what it is, the conversation is always about the hats. And that's cool with me. Because as long as it is, then I'm representing myself, my business, and the culture in the best way that I can.

That is one of the main reasons I wanted to write this book. Really, as a way to share my story, to break down some of the basics of hatting, introduce you to the concept of flairing, and then mix in some cigar pairings with my training as a cigar sommelier. When you bring all of these elements together in such a way you begin to realize the symmetry between them and how a lifestyle can be built around them. It's a beautiful thing when you can express yourself by the hat you're wearing as well as how you're wearing that hat. And how you wear that hat definitely matters.

Now, out of all of the hats that I currently have in my collection, I only have one bowler hat. But that's the thing, right? You gotta have a bowler in your arsenal if you're the Hat Ambassador. You know, if I ever need it or want to switch it up, I've got one that I can pull out and rock it. It's like, I try to have a least one hat of every style if possible and there's maybe only one or two that I don't currently have.

Hats and Cigars: Flairing and Pairing

But that's why I've covered these particular hats in this book. Because they are the most common hat styles that you're more than likely to come across. And again, that's part of the journey. At least, until I'm able to have every style of hat in my collection. Then…I might be able to say that the collection is complete.

The bowler, or sometimes referred to as a derby, is a hat that's made from a stiffened wool and has a rounded or "open" crown shape. When you see one, you know one. Bowlers have always been a semi-formal or casual styled hat and were predominantly worn by the working class going back to the late 19th century into the early 20th century.

Michael Brown

Hats and Cigars: Flairing and Pairing

Think, 1890's to 1920's, or so. You really don't see many bowlers being worn in today's hat culture. You've got to know a little something about the hat game if you're going to properly pull off a bowler.

Small feathers and even some small pins are best to use when flairing out a bowler in my opinion. A single Helmer hat feather and a Hats and Cigars Barber Pole Cigar Pin is all the flair that I need for my derby. It's just a hat that doesn't need much to style it. Hats like this are better suited style wise as a complement to your fit and doesn't necessarily have to be the centerpiece of what you're wearing. If you ask me, it always works well when worn with vintage styles and looks. You can use the same styling choices for both a boater and a bowler. It's a nice piece if you want to add some vintage swag to your collection.

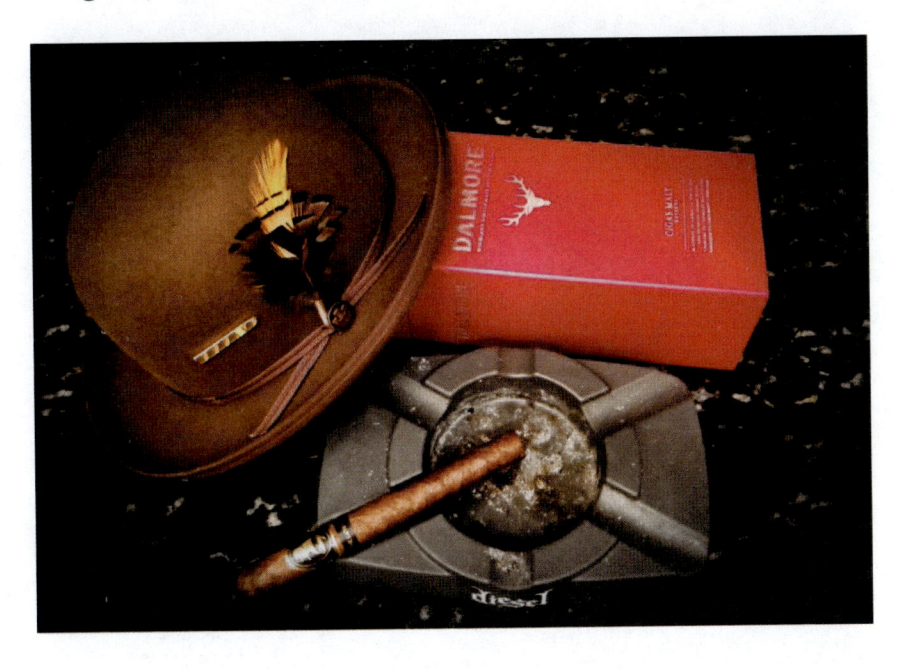

Michael Brown

"A cigar ought not to be smoked solely with the mouth, but with the hand, the eyes, and with the spirit."

-Zino Davidoff

When I read this quote, the first thing I think of is how much it correlates to an aspect of my cigar sommelier training which is the concept of tactile examination. Tactile examination is the act of fully examining the cigar prior to smoking it. So that means, with your eyes, your hands, even your ears, and lastly with your mouth, which is referred to as "cold tasting." Fully examining the cigar in this way can tell you many things about it even before you light it. And why not? I mean…if you're smoking something as fine as a premium hand rolled cigar you should treat it with the respect it deserves and take the time necessary to fully appreciate it for what it is.

The eyes are the first thing to be drawn to the beauty of a cigar. The many different shades and types of wrappers entices our interest to want to explore it even further. The hand is the first thing to touch a cigar. To feel and examine the entire construction from head to foot and therefore helping us to formulate out first impressions. The nose is the first thing to detect aromas and pick up on the subtle notes of a cigar. This is where our senses are heightened even more and beckons us to satisfy this desire by cutting it. The mouth is the first thing to taste the cigar. A cold draw will give you the last bit of stimulation needed before lighting it. Once the foot has been toasted, we are now fully prepared to indulge ourselves in an experience worthy of fulfilling our spirit.

If you're going to achieve such a heightened smoking experience, try smoking a cigar that is worthy of helping you achieve such goals. I'm talking about, none other than, the Davidoff Winston Churchill The Late Hour. Phenomenal stick! The barrel-aged tobaccos that are used, create a blend that's complex, yet smooth and full of flavor. One of the things that I love about this cigar is the how the pepper notes are layered throughout. I feel like I get coffee flavors too and definitely some creaminess mixed in there. The notes are subtle and don't get in the way of each other, but they come through just enough to make it a well-balanced medium to full strength cigar. Smooth all of the way through and amazing all by itself but when you pair it with something equally as exceptional, well, the only way that I can describe it is by calling it a masterpiece!

There's only one spirit that I even consider pairing with the Winston Churchill The Late Hour and that's just because, to me, there's no better spirit to pair it with. Allow me to introduce you to the Dalmore Cigar Malt Reserve. An exceptional spirit and my go-to if I'm enjoying a scotch whiskey.

Hats and Cigars: Flairing and Pairing

Now, when it comes to scotch, I'm by no means, in any way, as knowledgeable as I am with cognac. However, I do love to dabble every now and then, especially when it comes to pairing it with a nice Belvedere.

Scotch…I mean, I don't know…I've just always thought about scotch as a drink, like, you would have after dinner. A spirit that's best had after dark. You know…during the late hours of the night. Once you've carefully selected your smoking jacket for the evening and retired to "the study" type of vibe. Like, being surrounded by one of a kind art pieces, beautifully designed leather chairs, books galore, and deep soothing wood tones. Having a plethora of fine vintage hand-rolled cigars in the humidor to mull over and decide which one will it be tonight. Maybe it's just me…but anytime I think of scotch, that's what I think about. So, whenever I have the pleasure to enjoy some scotch, I want it to hold par with this exact same sentiment.

This pairing works on so many levels. Perfect in every way. The highlight, to me, is the balance between both the cigar and the scotch. The spiciness of The Late Hour blends beautifully with the smokiness of the Cigar Malt Reserve. In the first third of the cigar, the scotch has a slight "bite" to it but quickly finds its place within the pairing. As the cigar picks up a slight intensity in the 2nd and final thirds, the scotch mellows out and continues to blend in smoothly. Both elements of this pairing are full flavored and provide an array of flavors throughout the entire smoke. If you happen to consider yourself an aficionado or maybe even regarded as a connoisseur, then this is definitely a pairing truly worthy of such distinction.

Hats and Cigars: Flairing and Pairing

Michael Brown

Chapter 8: **Top Hats and Two-fingers**

"Some hats can only be worn if you're willing to be jaunty, to set them at an angle and to walk beneath them with a spring in your stride as if you're only a step away from dancing. They demand a lot of you."

-Neil Gaiman

Yes indeed, they do demand a lot of you. You know, one of the things about the hat game or being a hatter, is that you automatically stand out. Wherever you go. Whatever you're doing. Hat people feel themselves. You already show everyone by rocking a hat that you've got a sense of style and that you're proud to represent it. Your hat is an extension of your flyness and there's nothing wrong with embracing it.

The top hat is universally regarded as the quintessential formal hat. It makes me automatically think of tuxedos and tails type formal. You know, maybe even a cane and a monocle too. That's just me though. I'm talking about being dressed to the nines! White gloves even. That kind of formal. To me, it seems like the only way to do it. I mean…if you're going to wear a top hat, you've got to come correct. Everything on point from head to toe. And nothing says formal quite like a top hat.

I've only been to one black tie event. In my life. And this was only just recently. But let me tell you…this party was absolutely amazing! I had never been to any event quite like this. And I've been to a few shindigs if I don't say myself. But this one…this one was on a whole other level.

This event that I was invited to was the birthday celebration for Christine, a beautiful and prominent SOTL (Sister Of The Leaf) in the cigar culture. Yes…invite only! Now, let me just say…I was super surprised and even more honored just to get an invite to this exclusive party. It was a cigar event, a mansion party, and a wonderful celebration, all in one. It was nothing but A-listers and a who's who of the cigar culture. It was beautiful! And I had the pleasure of being there to experience it first-hand.

Hats and Cigars: Flairing and Pairing

The traditional and current modern styles of top hats are predominantly made from a hard black silk. Other materials used are wool, fur, and sometimes even leather. The tall flat crown of the top hat is its most recognizable and distinguishing feature. However, modern styles have shortened the crown as the culture has accepted wearing a top hat in more stylish ways than it was traditionally worn.

In today's hat culture, the top hat is being worn more and more as a casual style. Eccentric types and steam punks might be rocking a top hat. You might see creative types like musicians and artists wearing a top hat. Anyone with a sense of individuality and style may opt to add some flair to their look with a top hat. One thing's for sure, no matter what, you'll definitely stand out.

There's really not much you can do with a top hat in regard to flairing it out, in my opinion. It's kind of like a stand-alone hat. Meaning, it stands on its own in stature as just being a top hat. Nothing else needed. However, if you do want to add some flair to your top hat, make a big statement with big feathers. Whether in the top or through the side of the band, a top hat is tall enough and cool enough to handle those big feathers. The one top hat that I do have in my collection, I've flaired it out with just a Heartland hat pin and a Hats and Cigars Cigar Leaf Pin and that's it. But really, it doesn't even need any flair. The hat just speaks for itself.

Hats and Cigars: Flairing and Pairing

Michael Brown

Hats and Cigars: Flairing and Pairing

"The cigar is the perfect complement to an elegant lifestyle."

-George Sand

I've always looked at the cigar as a luxury product. What I mean by luxury is more about what luxury represents. You know, the things that make you feel like something is luxurious. Whether it's price or how rare it is or how exclusive it may be. Whether it's the time it takes to make it or if it's something that is totally hand made. Whether it might be a custom piece or a one-of-a-kind item. Whether it's the status attached to something or it's the status it brings to the person who has it. These are all just some examples of what I mean by luxury as it relates to cigars. Kind of like the same way with hats too though.

In a way, luxury can also mean, something that's reserved for special occasions. You know, those rare moments that may only happen every so often. The cigar has always been used to celebrate these special occasions. The birth of a child, a wedding or anniversary, or maybe reaching significant milestones in your life. Times like these calls for something more than the regular. Something special. Something that requires you to recognize just how meaningful that moment is. The type of cigar that will genuinely enhance these types of experiences can only be regarded as a luxury.

I feel like there's a certain amount of elegance associated with smoking a cigar. It's something about the experience of it all. There's a level of peace that comes with taking the time necessary to enjoy a fine cigar. From examining the cigar, to the dry tasting, to toasting it, and lighting it. This is all before even smoking it.

Michael Brown

Hats and Cigars: Flairing and Pairing

The time and effort put into the ritual of smoking a cigar is reserved to those who truly can appreciate exactly how elegant it is. Sometimes, it's the experiences that you have when you're smoking that make it elegant. Experiences like…rooftop soiree's, yacht parties, all-white affairs and black-tie events. All of these types of things are just so much more elegant when you add a cigar to the mix.

Once you have that perfect premium cigar to smoke, you'll always want to add an equally premium spirit to pair it with. Since we're talking spirits, there's a term I like to use called a "two-finger" pour. Originally used when speaking about bourbon only, but now the term can translate to all spirits.

Michael Brown

So, when I order a drink…it's cognac, two-fingers, on the rocks. That's how I take it. However, when I'm doing a pairing, I only want to have it "neat". Basically meaning, whatever spirit you're drinking, that it's not diluted or mixed with anything else. This is the best way to truly taste the spirit in the way that it was intended. Tasting the spirit neat is crucial for pairing because it allows you to better pair the notes between the spirit and the cigar.

"Who you wearin'? What you smokin'?"

I came up with the idea for this saying so I could use it anytime that I needed when I was at an event or anything like that. You know…like…anytime you watch one of those awards shows and all the celebrities walk the red carpet. The one thing that they always get asked when they get interviewed is, "who are you wearing?" So, I figured that would kind of be my thing. State what hat brand you're wearing and what cigar brand you're smoking…and make that a thing!

So, as I walk the red carpet for this final pairing, I'm proudly wearing the Goorin Bros. Cash Queen and I'm smoking the Jaime Garcia Reserva Especial 10th Anniversary Limited Edition 2019. The only thing I can think of that would make this any better is to pair it with something equally as special.

It doesn't get much more special than a limited, small batch release, that is soon to be a rare gem of a find. Let's just say, if you don't already have a bottle of this, then your chances of getting one may be slim to none. I'm talking about none other than, Hennessy Master Blender Selection No. 3. This expression from Hennessy is, by far, my favorite out of all 4 of the Master Blender's series, and the reason I wanted to include it in the book.

I remember being at a Hennessy Le Voyage master class tasting event. Our host was presenting the different expressions offered by Hennessy. He mentioned a new blend by Hennessy called the Master Blender Selection No. 3 and explained that it was comparable in quality and taste as Hennessy XO. I absolutely have to agree with this and it's why I think it pairs so well with the Jaime Garcia.

The Connecticut broadleaf wrapper of the 10th Anniversary is one of the main things that I'm drawn to on this cigar. It gives it a deep smokiness to the aroma and the taste. One of the things that I love about this stick is how smooth it is from start to finish. Kind of reminds me of, like, a creamy espresso with a subtle hint of sweetness. The smoke itself, even has a velvety smoothness to it which coats the palate. The Master Blender's Selection goes toe to toe with the Jaime on which one is the smoothest. Relatively no "burn" with the Hennessy or harshness with the Jaime on either finish. They both deliver with some complexity to them, but the highlight here is the rich flavors that you get from both the cigar and the cognac. The light fruitiness of the Hennessy and the dark tobacco notes of the Jaime Garcia dance back and forth between each other in a way that will give even the most discerning aficionado an unmatched experience in pure and total elegance!

When it comes to an elegant lifestyle, I have to believe that this can only be achieved by recognizing what elements are necessary to live that kind of life. You see...elegance only has its place in those where you make it so.

If you ask me...

You can never go wrong if your hat game is strong. Flair for days, in ways to give it that personal touch. Like a rocks glass pressing against your lips while sipping your favorite spirits. Smoking a Belvedere because it's clear, now, that that's what we're referring to. At least, that's what I'm talking about. I don't know about you. But that's why I wanted to write this. If I have to, I'll even recite this. Because I want to give something back to the game, to change and provoke a different frame of thought. Taken and seen through my eyes, through these words, and delivered to you with the upmost sincerest and deepest appreciation for what I so humbly refer to as this hats and cigars lifestyle!

Michael Brown

Chapter 9: Hats and Cigars

"A hat complements a cigar just as much as the cigar complements the person smoking it."

-The Hat Ambassador

It all just works together. In one beautiful harmonious way. They intertwine with each other to become a single glorious celebration. No two times being alike but every one of them is special in its own way. Leaving the interpretation up to the one who's doing it, or to the one who's seeing it be done. All of these elements complement each other like compliments from passersby. And they wonder why I always come this way. Every. Single. Day. It's like a symphony I listen to over and over. The notes bouncing up and down it's so melodic. If you've got it, then you know exactly what I'm saying. I'm just saying though. There's no better creation to culminate into such a beautiful experience the way that hats and cigars do. That's what I'm talking about!

Michael Brown

Hats and Cigars: Flairing and Pairing

123 | Page

Michael Brown

Chapter 10: **Lifestyle and Legacy**

"Keep a cigar in your grip, a drink at your lips, and a hat for your fit!"

-The Hat Ambassador

This is me! All day, every day. I say this quote often. It's my lifestyle...and it's my legacy! Believe that! It's the tag line for my brand. It's my motto. And, quite frankly, it doesn't get any better than this. If you ask me, there's not a better choice of words to express what this hats and cigars lifestyle is all about! Everything I believe in and stand for is in this quote. These are the three keys to the lifestyle. It's all about enjoying life. And in my opinion, there's no better way to enjoy it than this. Smoking a premium cigar, pairing it with a premium spirit, and wearing a premium hat to complete it all. Said by none other than yours truly...The Hat Ambassador!

I leave you with these words and share this as the last quote in this book, to humbly say thank you! Thank you to everyone who has helped me along the way and made this project possible. Thank you for the encouragement to step outside of my comfort zone and take on the challenge of writing this book. Thank you for believing in me and pushing me to do my best work. Thank you for the continued support of everyone who's out there rocking a Hats and Cigars pin on their hat. Thank you to all of the BOTL's and SOTL's. Thank you to the hat culture. To the cigar culture. Thank you for accepting me and allowing me to play just a small role in the big picture. The culture. That we love. I promise to represent it to the fullest, in the best way that I know how, every single day. Thank you from the bottom of my heart. This is truly a blessing.

When it's all said and done, I just hope that you enjoyed reading it as much as I enjoyed writing it!

Hats and Cigars: Flairing and Pairing

Michael Brown

About The Author

Who exactly is Mr. Michael Brown, the self-proclaimed Hat Ambassador, and the man behind one of the hottest new brands in the cigar culture?

The simple answer is...he's a gentleman. A brother. A father. A grandfather. A husband and friend. These are some of the obvious things that he is...but they don't even begin to scratch the surface or help you understand just who he is.

As someone who has dabbled in hats and cigars at different times in his life, it wasn't until he moved to Miami Beach in 2015 that both of these passions of his were able to come together and flourish, paving a path for who he is today.
In 2018, Michael successfully completed and received his certification as a cigar sommelier from the International Association of Cigar Sommeliers (IACS). His focus as a cigar sommelier is on the aspects of pairing cigars and spirits and more specifically, gourmet pairings. This will be one of the key features of this book and be highlighted throughout. His experience in the hat game can be credited to his years working for the hat company Goorin Bros. at their hat shop in Miami Beach since 2017. This is where he laid the foundation of becoming a professional hatter and it ultimately became a catalyst for him in starting his own brand, Hats and Cigars in 2019.

Hats and Cigars, the brand, was started by Michael to give cigar enthusiasts and hatters a product that wasn't previously available in the market. He had a vision and has made that vision a reality. His premium cigar-centric hat pins have changed the game when it comes to cigar and hat accessories. He continues to build his brand and grow the Hats and Cigars collection with premium pins and accessories for both hatters and cigar enthusiasts.

If you asked him, he would humbly refer to himself as a hat aficionado, a cigar enthusiast, a hat pin entrepreneur, and now hopefully, a soon to be best-selling author. So, now that you know a little about the author…there's nothing left to do but grab yourself a drink, light up a cigar, and immerse yourself in what could possibly be considered his greatest work to date.

Connect with The Hat Ambassador:

Facebook: Hats and Cigars
Instagram: @hatambassador
www.hatsandcigars.com

Denola M. Burton
DenolaBurton@EnhancedDNA1.com
www.EnhancedDNAPublishing.com

Made in the USA
Columbia, SC
09 May 2021